Solo Travel Tips for the Fearless Female Over Forty

By: Gaines Bishop

Editor: Jett Crisafulli

To my daughter, Tina, for all her encouragement.

To my nephew, Albert, without whose support this book would not have been possible.

Table of Contents

Introduction

Introduction

This guide was written to help you find ways and means to travel, as a woman over 40, to the places you have always wanted to go. Traveling solo is holding your life in your hands, knowing you can navigate this terrain on your own, making all your own decisions. While it can be a challenge at times, there is nothing that instills a sense of confidence and affords such adventure as travel. You meet more people if you travel solo, and therefore learn more about not only the people in the country you are visiting, but yourself at the same time.

Many of us like the freedom of backpacking, but we now want a bit more comfort and convenience. As I age, I have found I do not want to always have to carry a pack on my back. My current backpack has wheels and hidden straps.

However, too much convenience is counter to having a great adventure. When you have to manage your own trip, such as deciding where to go next, finding hotels and means of transportation, it gives you a sense of self-sufficiency you will never get by taking a tour where everything is done for you.

While I have backpacked for many years; I am really more of a "flashpacker" now. The first question on many travelers' lips may well be - what is flashpacking? Who are these mysterious *flashpackers*?

Flashpacking is really just a term used to describe a fairly old way of traveling. Many flashpackers are actually just the growing number of "techno-travelers" out there. They have smart phones and digital cameras. They're traveling with their laptops and/or tablets. They may want to blog about their travel experiences, or just keep up with their social media page - they want WiFi at their hostel or guesthouse. So as you see, a flashpacker is essentially just the usual backpacker or independent traveler, looking for something a bit more upscale from their lodgings and mode of travel. For instance, they would rather take a $100 flight than a 24 hour bus ride.

They want all the flexibility of the independent traveler with an unfixed itinerary which allows you to think on your feet and go wherever your fancy takes you. Although they don't want your standard budget hotel; they're after the advantages of a good old-fashioned cheap hostel, with just a bit more, well, luxury. And even the most hardcore backpackers among us can do with a bit of luxury from time to time.

A good guidebook like Lonely Planet is good to have so you may start reading months in advance, have time to decide on the places you want to see, and things you want to do. The guide also gives you not only transportation information, but places to stay and things to see. You can't see the entire country, nor would you want to travel that fast. As Americans, we think we have to have every minute filled with all the best sights, and end up with an itinerary so full that you never have time to learn about the culture you are visiting. I have been known to throw out my itinerary by the third day and simply "wing it".

So slow down and enjoy your trip. You don't have to see everything; just see the things that truly interest you and meet as many of the locals and other travelers as you can. Strike up a conversation with people you don't know and make new friends. Really experience the place and culture, and as you learn about the new country, you will find you learn more about yourself as well.

As a young girl, I always wanted to travel. I would request information on other countries and when it arrived by mail, I would study all the information received and dream of being there. I always wanted to see the Taj Mahal (I cut a photo of it from a magazine and put it on my wall) and as I stood beside the actual Taj Mahal, at 60 yrs. of age, I realized that although it had taken many years to arrive, I had held onto my dream and finally accomplished it. That feeling was like none other!

I can't emphasize enough how empowering solo travel is. I have been all the way around the world, to 20 countries on five continents, and the few times I had a travel companion were not near as gratifying as going solo. I never feel so alive as when I travel. Who travels solo at my age? I do!

Gaines Bishop

Chapter 1

Is Travel a Priority?

"Thirty years from now, you will be more disappointed by the things that you didn't do than by the ones you did do. So throw off the bowlines. Sail away from the safe harbor. Catch the trade winds in your sails. Explore. Dream." *Mark Twain*

Please don't allow yourself to believe that you can't travel due to finances, work, or responsibilities. Remember the old adage - where there is a will, there is a way! Although we get caught up in our day-to-day lives, we need to also follow our passion. If that passion for you is travel, hopefully I can show you a way not only to travel, but to do it on the cheap.

Priorities are the key here! To be able to travel, you must make it one of your priorities. That may mean making a few sacrifices in daily life. Sometimes you may need to ask yourself when you go to buy something, do you actually need it? Is it more important than your trip? Wouldn't you rather spend the money on travel? Exploring new and exotic places on this marvelous earth is priceless. So, think about the value of your hard-earned money and the quality of your life. Spending on travel far exceeds acquiring more stuff.

There are several easy and obvious ways to build a travel fund, whether it is in the bank, on PayPal, or in a jar on the shelf. You will probably be less tempted to pull funds if it is not easy to access. At one point, I sold a lot of my belongings to travel for six months in India. What a trip! Sell things on craigslist.org or eBay.com, things that you have stored, or things laying around that you don't use anymore. Or gather it all up and have a garage sale. Put all that money in your new travel fund. Put your company bonus in your travel fund. Save a regular amount each paycheck, even if it is not a lot. If you have a savings account, transfer a set amount from your checking account as soon as you get paid. You will never miss it. Get a second or part-time job for a while and save the entire check. Before long, you will have money for your trip. Make your heart's desire for travel your goal, and nothing can stop you!

When bearing in mind your travel goals and destinations, something critical to consider is that the travel industry makes a lot more money from travelers going to certain countries. Research the countries you want to visit and carefully compare the costs of travel to each destination. For example, if you want to go to France, consider Prague; it is much less expensive. Western/central Europe is more costly to visit than eastern Europe and has the same wonderful architecture Instead of Spain, go to South America. Instead of Japan or China, go to Thailand. And of course, India is very inexpensive! Want to see the Sahara Desert? Try Morocco instead of Egypt. Think hotels, food, shopping, travel within the country, etc. and you will find that these will be much less expensive. The price of the ticket to some of these countries may be higher, but the money you save in general travel costs will significantly off-set the ticket price and you can stay longer!

If you cannot get time off from your job other than for your 2-week vacation, think about a visit to South America. It is close and the time zone is similar to that of the U.S. - no time spent with jet lag. Want to go to the Amazon? You do not need to go to Brazil because Ecuador has the Upper Amazon Basin. You can have an amazing adventure trip down the Rio Napo (a large tributary to the Amazon), in a dugout canoe and hike the rain forest. Does lounging on a warm, sandy beach warm your traveler's heart? You don't need Hawaii or the South Pacific when the beaches of Mexico are so close. Be flexible, be creative, and you will discover many other ways and means to do what you want.

As you can see, creativity and flexibility are the secrets to successful travel. If you are open to new ideas and non-conventional thinking when it comes to travel opportunities, you will be surprised at the doors that will open, providing you with ways to travel on your own terms and within your own budget. For example, you've heard of the term "the road less traveled". When in a foreign country, visit areas off the beaten path. It will be less expensive, you will run into fewer tourists, and have more adventures. Visit neighborhoods and enjoy meals at small, local cafes. You will experience firsthand the flavor of a country and the culture of the people. Take a walking tour, go by bicycle, camel, freighter, or take a kayak tour. Here's an idea: buy a horse and travel horseback - you can sell it before you leave! Seek off-beat accommodations: monasteries, convents, ashrams, camping, or home-stays (see more on this in Chapter 6).

Do you find yourself taking a trip to see relatives

because it's expected, or are you traveling to the same places every vacation? Think about taking a trip somewhere new for less money than it costs to drive or fly across the U.S., paying for motels, gas, and food along the way. You will be fulfilling YOUR OWN dreams, opening a whole new world of amazing experiences.

When it comes to children, and it's not an option to send them to grandma's or to visit other relatives, you might be surprised at how easy and enjoyable it is to bring them along for exciting trips to foreign lands. I have witnessed Western families in India with very small children, enjoying all the new sights and sounds together! Imagine your children fascinated by watching elephants on the street and monkeys swinging from tree to tree! Again, creativity and flexibility are the keys, but worth every effort in providing children with the priceless, life-enriching education that only first-hand travel can provide.

If you really want to travel, if it's a passion burning in your soul, make it a goal, a priority, and don't let anything stop you! No one to travel with? Solo travel is very empowering! You don't need anyone to agree with your passion, it is YOUR passion. If I could give all of you would-be travelers advice, I would say one thing to you – Don't wait - GO!

Chapter 2

Preparations

"Tourists don't know where they've been, travelers don't know where they're going." *Paul Theroux*

Preparing for your trip is half the fun of going, but there are several things to consider. Below is a list of some of the most important items you won't want to neglect. Nothing is worse than getting to a border with an expired visa! For example, upon re-entering Egypt, the official at the border going from Israel into Egypt discovered my visa had expired. I did not realize at the time that your visa time-line starts when they insert the visa into your passport - not when you enter the country. By developing a rapport with the officials, I was able to get them to help me. One of them got out his own cell phone and called an official who was willing to come to the border station, on a Sunday, to sign a letter to vouch for me and I obtained another visa for the remainder of my trip.

- Do you need a visa before entering the country?

Find out by going to the country's official website. It may require several weeks or more to obtain, so allow plenty of time. A lot of countries give you a visa at the airport or border (be sure it is an official border crossing, not just a town on the border) when you enter the country. Be sure it is for the length of time you want to spend in the country. If they allow three months, but only give you a stamp for 30 days, address it right then and there. Most agents are very amenable to your requirements.

-If you want travel insurance, be sure to check to see if it covers everything you want such as evacuation in a medical emergency, reimbursement for a doctor's visit or hospital in another country, a trip delay due to illness, lost luggage, etc. It is better to have it and not need it, than to need it and not have it. However, buying insurance is a personal preference. I broke a bone and ripped ligaments in my foot hiking in the Himalayas. I went to the emergency room to have x-rays, then saw an orthopedist for a cast - all for $20. I then flew home to have my own doctors follow-up. I was lucky it was a minimal charge as I had opted for no insurance

-At least 6 weeks ahead of your trip, check with the local health department travel nurse for vaccination requirements. You may also need malaria pills for some countries.

-Email a copy of your vital information to yourself: tickets, itinerary, visa, passport, credit/debit cards, front and back. You can easily print them out in an internet shop if needed.

-Stop the newspaper while you are away and arrange for mail pick-up, or have the post office hold it until you return.

-Arrange for pet care, house-sitting, and plant care. If you will be gone for an extended period, arrange to have your car driven at least once a month.

-Leave a copy of your itinerary with a trusted friend...just in case!

-Learn a few words in the language of your destination country. It will be greatly appreciated by the locals!

-Make a list of things to do in your home before leaving. For example, unplug small appliances (toaster, TV, etc.) for safety!

-Get a current guidebook whether you take a tour or travel solo. You will want to read about your destination before arriving.

-Download everything you want to take on your tablet or computer- music, movies, photos. You will want to show others your photos from home, listen to familiar music in your room, or watch a movie on a night bus or train.

-If planning to carry a phone, will it work overseas? A phone you acquire from a carrier, such as AT&T is coded or locked to that carrier. In order to use another carrier's SIM card, you must unlock your phone. If you are under contract with the carrier, they will not unlock it, so you may need to use a different phone. If you are not under contract, but are using a phone service provider, they will tell you how to unlock it. You can also buy unlocked phones online. Using a foreign SIM card (you will see signs to buy it there) will save a significant amount of money as opposed to your phone provider's plan.

-Do a search for blogs on the country you will visit. They can be a great source of inside information. Read a bit of each one to see if it fits your style, then dive in and learn!

-Look over your proposed itinerary and remember, it is not set in stone. Try to travel at a slower pace so you can soak up the local culture and meet more people. Besides, packing and unpacking every couple of days is tiring. You may not see every tourist attraction in the country, but you will see more in other ways. I have been invited to parties, dinners, and even to a wedding just by socializing with local folks!

Chapter 3

Cultural Differences

"To travel is to discover that everyone is wrong about other countries." *Aldous Huxley*

Let me start by saying that we are not all that different from others - we marry, have children, work, play, and want to be happy like all people anywhere in the world.

- When you enter a country, you agree to live temporarily by its customs and rules, so it helps to read about the culture before leaving home. Some of them may seem strange or even objectionable, but as travelers our aim is to experience the culture, not change it. For example, they may cook eggs differently than you would at home...enjoy the differences. Let go of judgments regarding foreign customs. Things are not good or bad, just different. No one drives on the wrong side of the road; in some countries they drive on the left, and in some on the right. While we may not understand their customs, such as religion, hygiene, style of dress, or dining practices, it is their country and we might enjoy our visit more if we relax and appreciate the differences.

-People in Latin America tend to move in more closely during conversation due to a different sense of personal space. Others often operate with a concept of time that may be different than your own; relax and go with the flow.

-Wear clothes according to the custom of the country. That may mean just covering your head when visiting temples, or taking off your shoes before going into a temple or even a home. If you see a stack of shoes outside, deposit yours there, then enter. They may even require your legs to be covered. At the Royal Palace in Bangkok, they will loan you a sarong if needed.

-Practice being observant during social interactions, then model your behavior after those around you. Taking photos is not always permitted, even if no sign is posted. I was in a Shiite temple while a service was being conducted, snapped a photo. I was quickly approached and told photos were not allowed.

-When observing festivals or rituals, don't join in without an invitation, especially if it is religious in nature.

The smile is universal.

My Peace Corps Experience
Nicaragua 1996-1998

On my 50th birthday I took a long look at my life. I felt like I had accomplished a lot and started thinking about giving something back. Over the next few months, I read about the U.S. Peace Corps and decided to join. It would enable me to fulfill several long-time goals: help others, experience personal growth, learn Spanish, and live in a Latin American country.

I arrived in Nicaragua with a group of 24 volunteers. After three days in Granada for orientation, we were assigned to the site where we would live for the next two years. After three months staying with a local family in our site, and attending 4-6 hours of classes daily, we were sworn in as volunteers. Our Peace Corps swear-in ceremony was conducted in the offices of the president of the country, Doña Violeta Barrios de Chamorro, on Nov. 29, 1996. What an exciting day with this charming woman, and it was televised as well on the local channel. We then went to our respective sites - mine was the city of Masaya, where I was fortunate enough to find a wonderful old Spanish-style house to rent.

When they assigned me to the United Nations Project, I was quite excited. During the next two years I worked on several projects. I organized and taught business skill workshops, photographed artisan products in all parts of the country for display on the Web, wrote a website with a catalog of products to facilitate exportation, and secured a server to donate space for the site. I conducted training classes at the university in Managua in basic internet use for the employees of the U.N. Project. In Masaya, I designed logos, brochures, and business cards for artisan groups and cooperatives, and instituted Junior Achievement classes in the local high schools in the state.

Another volunteer and I worked with a group of 25 women who fished Lake Nicaragua. We wrote two grants for the money to construct five boats with accompanying 50-ft. drift nets, and to purchase a freezer to store the fish until they could get them to market. We also conducted various business seminars and helped the group form a co-op and communal bank.

I was a member of the Peace Corps Women in Development Committee and completed service Sept. 1, 1998. It was an experience that, as one volunteer put it, "would test my mettle" - it did!

Yes, it was the toughest job I'll ever love. It's not for everyone, but I recommend it highly. I know I learned much more than I ever taught.

Chapter 4

Traveling Smart & Light

"As you think, you travel, and as you love, you attract. You are today where your thoughts have brought you; you will be tomorrow where your thoughts take you." *James Lane Allen*

Make a packing list, print it out, and check it off! The more times you pack, the easier it becomes. You will develop your packing skills before you know it. I recommend you start a week before - this gives you time for things to pop into your head, and to purchase items you don't already have. You can look online for the weather in your destination or check your guidebook. This makes it easier to pack the right clothes and shoes.

-Set out your suitcase in your bedroom. As you run across small things you may want to take, drop them in your open bag. When you do the final packing, you can then decide if you want to take everything or not.

- Do laundry the day before packing so your

favorite things are clean.

-Lay everything out on the bed and check to see if each piece of clothing goes with everything else. For example, does the shirt go with all the pants? Or is everything patterned? Pick a base color - green or blue? Brown or black? If done this way, you will be able to carry fewer clothes as they will all mix and match! Remember, jeans may be your favorite, but they are heavy and dry slowly. I only take one pair. Solid colors blend in and no one notices it's the same clothes you wore the day before. Earth tones do not show dust and dirt as much as some colors. Think of dirt roads and flying dust.

-Take clothes that travel well – especially underwear that can be washed and hung for quick dry. I carry a small clothes line for this purpose. I also carry a quick-dry shirt in case.

-Don't pack or wear expensive jewelry. Wear silver or costume jewelry in a style that will go with everything so you don't have to carry extra and constantly be deciding what to wear. Remember, you will be traveling in a poor country where theft is more common, and you do not want to be a walking target.

- If you take meds, be sure you have enough to

make it through the trip. Check with your doctor to get advance prescriptions for travel and fill them before departing. Make a copy of the prescription in case you are questioned at the airport about the pills.

-Get out your Ziploc bag...here is a quote from the airlines:

"3-1-1 for carry-ons. Liquids, gels, aerosols, creams and pastes must be 3.4 ounces (100ml) or less per container; must be in 1-quart-sized, clear, plastic, zip-top bag; 1 bag per passenger placed in screening bin".

-Put items that may affect other things in your bag, such as shoes or bathing suits that have been in chlorine, in Ziploc bags.

-What about electronics? Do you have all the right cords to recharge your phone, tablet or computer, camera? Always double check, as you would be challenged to find them in some countries. You will need a plug converter, which can be different depending on which part of the world you're visiting, but I suggest purchasing a universal one. You can find these online or at stores like R.E.I. (Recreational Equipment International).

- Are you checking a backpack or bag? Or can

you make it with just a carry-on with wheels? Remember, less is better, especially when it all goes on your back and/or you have to carry it. At times there are long staircases where you must carry your bag yourself or hire a porter, such as at a train station. Another option is to buy a bag with wheels and hidden backpack straps.

-Weigh your bag after packing - is it over the limit? Check the airlines website for baggage limits. And you will want extra room to bring back souvenirs. Another other option is to take a nylon bag that packs flat, to carry home the items from your shopping trip! If it is close to the holidays, you can shop for much less money, and the gifts will be more unusual.

-If you want to carry a backpack, read about them before buying. Some of them offer wheels and straps! If you have a store like R.E.I. close by, they will show you how to get the best fit, which is very important. If not, they have great instructions for buying packs, sleeping bags, etc. on their website. Purchase the best one you can afford as they last many, many years, have features the cheap ones don't have, and are much more durable. Mine is going on 10 years old and still looks new - no holes or duct tape!

- Do you have emergency information both on

the outside and inside of your bags? If you have a friend where you are visiting, or the hotel name and address where you will stay when arriving, put their name, address and phone number *inside* the bag as well.

-Prepare for a lot of waiting time for buses, trains, planes, and other people to arrive. Did you pack a book or have plenty on your tablet to read? How about your music? Got earbuds?

-Be earth-friendly and take a refillable personal water bottle. You can carry it through security if it is empty, but use only bottled water on the plane.

-Lock your bags, carry-on bags included. Look online or in a travel store for TSA-approved locks. The TSA has keys to open those locks in case they need to further inspect the bag. Nylon zip-ties are a good alternative to locks. If they are inspecting your bag, it will be cut and there should be a note left inside from TSA.

- You can buy anything you really need overseas -maybe not a familiar brand - but don't over pack! Check out some good websites like onebag.com.

Bonus Tip! You can almost always gate check baggage (unless it's abnormally large). Take two large carry-ons and ask them to check one at the gate. It's free and I never pay fees. This is great when you return with your extra bag from that shopping spree!

Packing List

This is a general packing list of things you may want to take, depending on the weather and your personal preference. Some of these are optional, and remember, all liquids must fit in, and be carried in a 1-quart Ziploc bag. You cannot carry sharp metal items, or batteries in your carry-on. I have listed what I carry, in a carry-on, for six months of travel (be prepared to purchase refills):

-Passport & Ticket

- Money Belt (wear under your clothes)

-Credit Cards (2 only) If something happens, you have only lost one and the other is at your hotel

-Cell Phone (unlocked) Call your cell provider to unlock your phone for you

-Camera (if you have a good quality phone camera, that might do as well)

- * Batteries, if needed

-Memory Cards for computer, electronics, camera. (I buy 32 mg cards to hold as much as possible)

- Universal plug converter

-Charging cords for all electronics

-Extension Cord (handy if the plug-in is out of the way, or there is only one)

-Flashlight/Torch (to see during a power outage, and check under the bed before checking out)

- Padlock, medium size

- Guidebook (latest edition)

- Sunglasses

-Compass (if navigating by a map, this comes in handy)

- Water Bottle (that does not leak)

- Cleansing Wipes

- Hand Sanitizer

-Cosmetics/Shaving Gear/Toiletries (in a 1-quart Ziploc)

-First Aid Kit (Meds for stomach & intestinal problems, Band-aids, antibiotic ointment, pain reliever, ace bandage, Benadryl, and whatever else you need)

- Prescription Meds (enough for your trip)

-Tampons (some countries don't have them)

- Hair Dryer (if not for style, it may be cold)

- Brush & Comb

-Shower Cap (handy for a quick shower when you don't want to wash your hair)

-Ear Plugs (2 pair as they are easy to lose and we need our sleep)

- *Small Manicure set, Tweezers, Nail Clipper

- *Scissors w/Cork on the tip

- Mending Kit

- Sink Stopper (flat rubber for laundry in the sink)

-Sleep Sack/Bag (I carry a silk sleep sack as I don't camp)

- Swim Suit (even if you are going to the Arctic)

-Pants – three pairs total or two pairs and one dress or skirt (Wear your most comfortable on the plane)

-Tops – five tops, one light sweater and one camisole (that works as an under layer for outdoors and under a jacket for a dressier look).

-Underwear - five pair

- Heavy Socks - five pair (can double as slippers)

- Comfortable Walking Shoes and/or hiking boots

- Sandals for a warm climate

- Pajamas or a nightie

-One cardigan OR light jacket that can dress up or down depending on jeans or pants and accessories

- Flip-Flops

-One scarf to dress up casual clothes (many uses from head cover to beach cover-up, something to sit on to protection from a wind storm)

- Pocket-size Notebook (so handy)

- Tablet or Reading Light

- Book, Paperback, or eBooks

- Pen/Pencil

- *Swiss Army Knife

- Tissues, small packet

- Toilet Paper (in zip-lock with core removed, pull

from center)

-Travel Alarm (or use phone, watch, or tablet)

-Umbrella (as small as you can get - good for rain or hot sun)

- Towel & Washcloth (travel type that dry fast)

- Ziploc bags in several sizes

- Eye Mask

Sounds like a lot but it's not; it all fits in my carry-on. Rinse clothes out when necessary or send to laundry.

* Cannot carry in carry-on.

Chapter 5

Planes, Trains, and Buses

"Airplane travel is nature's way of making you look like your passport photo." *Al Gore*

I have met the most interesting people, local and other travelers, when getting from point A to point B by different modes of transportation. I have met a therapist from Canada, the supervisor of a local phone company, a mountain climber from Switzerland, an Italian woman who owns a cave in Cappadocia, Turkey, plus a lot of Europeans and local families. I keep in touch with some of these people today.

Planes:

-Consider going during the "shoulder season" - the month before and the month after the tourist season for the best prices on both flights and hotels. There are also fewer tourists.

-Research the best fares before buying. The same flight can vary in price from website to website. Check in Chapter 16 - Resources page for websites.

-Be sure to join the airline's frequent flyer program, as those miles add up and you will eventually have a free trip.

-Start about three to six months ahead for the best flights at the cheapest rates. While you may be able to get a cheap flight later, you will most likely have long layovers. Don't forget to go to the airline website for your flight and reserve your seats.

-Check-in 24 hours before your flight. If flying domestic, you can print your boarding passes as well. If you print them on another color paper, it will be easier to locate them at the gate.

-Book internal/domestic flights at your destination country with local airlines, as they are usually much cheaper.

-When dressing to travel, go for comfort! That's everything from your shirt, to your shoes, to your underwear. It can get cold on planes, trains, and buses, so carry a light-weight fleece with you, even if your destination has a hot climate.

-You will want to take off your shoes at the checkpoints in the airport, as well as when seated, so if you are wearing your sport shoes or hiking boots, tie them loose so you can slip them on and off easily.

-For those long trips, bring a pre-pasted disposable toothbrush to use right before arrival. You will feel fresh and ready for the new place!

-Pressurized airplane cabins are dehydrating, so drink plenty of water or other liquids. Avoid caffeine and alcohol as they will further dehydrate you.

Trains:

-Some websites will let you reserve trains in a foreign country, in case you need a train right away when you arrive and are not sure you can get a seat.

-If you are going to a country such as India, try to read a bit about the trains ahead of your trip so you can figure them out when you need one. Try IndiaMike.com for a ton of information on India. Seniors get a 40% discount on trains!

-On a train it is possible for someone to get on at a stop while you sleep, take your whole bag, then get right back off before the train continues. Lock it to something with a cable lock to sleep more soundly.

-It is nice to combine food with others in your train compartment to make a more complete meal. If your mates are locals, they will have local foods you may enjoy and they will appreciate the things you brought that will be unusual for them.

-Always take at least a snack and water when on the road. You never know when you might be able to get something to eat. You can also get a sandwich to-go from a restaurant, or buy fruit, nuts, bread, and chocolate - things that are good to share.

-I like to purchase a bag of balloons before I leave as you cannot always find them in poorer countries. They are perfect for those times when babies cry or children are unruly on a bus or train. Simply go to their seats, blow one up, and hand it to them. Leave it soft if giving to a baby so it doesn't burst and scare them. Before you know it, there will be balloons bouncing around between passengers, both children and adults!

Buses:

- Most third world countries have long-distance buses that are usually equipped with beds/berths and travel overnight. You save one night's hotel fare as a bonus!

-In a lot of Latin American countries you get a senior discount for buses - remember to ask when purchasing.

-Most buses do not have a toilet, while trains do...something to consider when deciding which to take.

-Long-distance buses sometimes stop for toilet breaks where there aren't any toilets available. If you are a woman you may want to wear something that can cover you a bit as you may have to "go" in a field in front of others! One time we stopped next to a vacant area, no bushes or trees, and we all had to relieve ourselves in front of everyone else! I was glad it was dark.

Chapter 6

Hotels, Hostels, & Home Stays

"Travel, in the younger sort, is a part of education; in the elder, a part of experience." *Francis Bacon*

Your hotel or guesthouse is so important. It is your refuge after a day's activities, so you want to be sure it is a place you like to be.

-For some reason, they like to put solo travelers in a room not much bigger than a walk-in closet! Always ask to see the room before paying. I was once put in a room that was triangular, in the corner of the first floor. When I refused it, they moved me to a room that was large, with split bamboo on the walls, an ornately carved bed, and a balcony. The price was the same! NEGOTIATE - especially if it is the off-season, as prices can greatly vary.

-Do you have a reservation at a hotel for the first couple of nights? You want to be sure you have a place to stay after a long, tiring trip. Going to the other side of the world? Book 2-3 days to recover from the jet-lag. And remember - as we age it takes longer to adjust. Don't rush yourself!

-When I land in a large city upon arrival in a new country, I want more comfort (room service, nice bed & bath, AC, flat-screen TV), as I will be in the room most of the time to get accustomed to the new time zone. Other times, I am good with a simple private room with bath. It is whatever you prefer and what your budget allows.

-A lot of rooms in guesthouses have a hasp and padlock on the door. For better security, bring a medium size padlock of your own to use. One time I came back to my room and two guys were in it! The key to their padlock somehow fit mine and they walked right in. It is better to use your own to be sure the key is uniquely yours.

-If staying for awhile and you need your room cleaned while there, you will have to either leave your key at the desk, or be in the room while they are cleaning. Anytime you leave your key, be sure your money belt is on you.

-When going out and you do not want to wear your money belt, lock it in your luggage/backpack **if** you have your own padlock on the door! If you do not have your own lock on the door, do not try to hide it in the room as the hotel employees know the rooms better than you. Some places have a safe either at the front desk or in the room, which is handy. If not, wear your money belt!

-Pick up a business card the first time you leave your hotel. You can show it to the taxi driver to get back or to someone for directions.

-It's a good idea to have extra copies of your passport and visa for smaller places, IE: guesthouses and home-stays, as they may not have a copier. This way you can keep your passport with you rather than let them keep it for copying and returning later. I made color copies and they re-copied them in black & white. I have no idea why!

-Dorms are, of course, the least expensive as most do not have a bath attached and you will be sleeping in a room with several other people. It all depends on your budget and the amount of comfort you desire at that time. The bath may only have cold water, or hot water only during certain hours - always ask! As I age, I find I want more amenities and someone to carry my pack upstairs. I even bought a pack with wheels last time I traveled. My back appreciates it!

-You can arrange your own home-stay or have an agency arrange one for you. Usually you will find them in your guidebook or check the Resources page of this book. Sometimes the tourism office books them as well.

Definitions:

Home-stay - This is when you stay in a local family's home. You may or may not have much privacy as you may have to share a room, or even a bed, with their child/children, or they may have a private room for you. The bath and toilet may not be what you are used to either, and you may be expected to work a bit. Before you book it, clarify the arrangements.

Hostel - A hostel provides budget-oriented, sociable accommodation where guests can rent a bed in a dormitory and share a bathroom, lounge and sometimes a kitchen. Rooms can be mixed or single-sex, although private rooms are usually available as well. These accommodations are made for guest interaction as opposed to hotels that are engineered to give their guests the utmost in privacy. You meet travelers in the communal area, which is a good way to hear about interesting places you may have otherwise missed. The kitchen can be a money saver as you can cook some of your own meals.

Guest house/guesthouse - In some parts of the world a guest house is similar to a hostel, bed and breakfast, or inn where in other parts of the world, guest houses are a type of inexpensive hotel-like lodging. In still others, it is a private home which has been converted for the exclusive use of guest accommodation. The owner sometimes lives in an entirely separate area within the property.

Peru & Bolivia, South America

There are not enough words to aptly describe the beauty and fascinating history of South America. It's a continent that offers endless intrigue and adventure such as I briefly describe in this excerpt from my personal journal:

"After I arrived in Lima, I took an early flight out the next morning to Cuzco. After two days there to get accustomed to the altitude, I caught the local bus to the Sacred Valley of Urubamba. I spent three days exploring the Inca ruins of Pisac and Ollantaytambo, then hopped the train to Aguas Calientes, a small village at the edge of the cloud forest where Machu Picchu perches on a peak above.

I was traveling alone and was glad to meet Jorge from Argentina and Julio from Brazil who had just hiked the Inca Trail - a four-day, three-night trek, through two very high mountain passes, that ends at Machu Picchu. We spent the next two days exploring the ruins, climbing Huaynu Picchu - the tall peak behind the ruins, and passing the evenings in the hot springs. Time to leave always came too soon and, after a four hour ride to Cuzco, we parted ways.

Discovering there wasn't a train to Puno, my next destination, for another day, I spent my time between the airline cargo office trying to recover the articles missing from my bag, and visiting the museums. Puno, the main Peruvian port on Lake Titicaca, was a ten-hour train ride. Arriving in Puno, I checked into a guest house. I awoke early the next day to the sounds of vendors setting up their stands in the street below. Grabbing a couple of rolls from the bakery next door, I hiked to the top of the hill (is this what you call another peak at 11,000 feet?). There's a tall statue of Manco Capac, the first Inca, overlooking the medium-size town and the large Lake Titicaca.

After lunch, I booked a tour of the ruins at Sillustani, 30 minutes northwest of Puno. By 3:00 p.m., I was on a bus to the funerary towers that overlook the lake. The guide, Norka, was great! Not only did you get a tour, but she gave a thorough history of the dignitaries buried in the huge towers, some of which predated the Incas. A woman and her daughter herded llama and cattle through the ruins. She wielded a leather slingshot above her head, throwing rocks to scare the animals back to the desired area.

In the morning I headed for the docks and the islands of Uros, Amantani and Taquile. The boat was nice and held several natives, a Norwegian couple and their 3-year-old son, a German man, Andres, a Philippine woman named Stephanie, a Greek couple, and myself. We stopped first in Uros, the only floating islands in the world. The Uros Indians live in houses made of reeds, have tortoro boats made of reeds, and indeed the entire island is made of reeds! As the reeds rot on the bottom, they pick up the houses and lay more reeds on top - a pretty incredible sight.

Next, we stopped at the island of Amantani where we were to be for the next 24 hours. Stephanie and I decided to stay together in a home with a Quechua family, who served fried potatoes with rice upon our arrival and a lunch of potato soup. We shared one of the six rooms in the two-story dwelling that overlooked the lake. After walking around the town (a plaza, two stores and a church) to take photos, I sat with the grandfather while he made rope from reeds, and talked as the sun set behind the mountains of Bolivia in the distance. I felt as if I could stay in this tranquility forever, but then there was the fact that they had no electricity, no running water, an outhouse with a hole in the floor, and they seemed to have nothing to eat but the potatoes and rice we had for lunch, dinner and breakfast. Morning found us headed for Taquile for a half day, then back on the boat to return to Puno.

The next day, Stephanie and I decided to travel together and caught the bus to Copacabana, Bolivia. After crossing the border, the roads changed from pavement to a hand-laid stone highway. Copacabana is a quaint town on the south coast of the lake. It's the port for boats to the Islands of the Sun and Moon, the sacred islands of the Incas. There's a stone path leading up the hill to the east with the twelve stations of the cross at intermediate levels culminating in a mountaintop temple overlooking the lake and facing the sunset. There are twelve stone altars atop, and upon my arrival there at 6:30 a.m., I discovered a local man in a typical Peruvian hat, conducting a healing ceremony for five locals in Quechua. I stood to the side as he sprinkled incense in an antiquated burner and touched the sick woman to heal her. I felt as if a photo would be intrusive and took none.

That afternoon there was a street festival to practice for the one due the following month. The women swirled in their heavy brocade skirts with multiple petticoats, silk shawls with lavish fringe, black bowler hats and black flat shoes. The afternoon turned to night as the brass band played and they danced from one end of town to the other. Around 10:00 p.m. the party was over and there was silence as they abandoned the streets for their homes.

At 8:30 the next morning we were off to the Isla del Sol on the most pitiful boat I have ever seen. The boards we sat on weren't nailed down, the engine compartment stood open so the captain could tweak the motor as needed and there were no life vests. Our captain had obviously been to the party the night before as he was still drunk. Two passengers took over the boat as he finally passed out below deck. We headed across the lake toward the island, a good four hours away. There are some small ruins on the north side of the island, but not much else, as the Sun Gate monument was moved from the island and now stood in the plaza in Copacabana.

The following morning, Stephanie continued her trip through Bolivia and I caught the bus back to Puno, then boarded the train that makes its way over the altiplano to Cuzco. One more night there, and I flew to Lima for a day and a half of last minute shopping and museums. The Museo de

Oro (Gold Museum) was fantastic, with a three-room vault full of gold masks, clothing trimmed in gold, and jewelry. There was actually an entire wall made of a sheet of gold! There were more rooms of ancient pottery, tools and tapestries. It represented several cultures predating the Incas. Unfortunately, most of the Inca gold was stolen by the Spaniards in the early 1500's."

As you can see, it was a fascinating trip but the three weeks certainly flew. South America is a wonderful place to explore with as much adventure as you can stand - go and enjoy!

Chapter 7

Safe Passage

"Adventure means learning, it means encountering things you could not foresee and figuring out how to address them - finding some way to get through it, if it's scary, or just being novel in your approach if it's a common obstacle. Adventure is a creative process. When you put yourself in a place that's totally different, you reveal yourself to yourself." *Unknown*

Of course, we all want to stay safe, and the best way to do that is to be informed. Read about your location for areas that may not be safe - don't go there! Ask locals before you take that hike to the top of the hill - is it safe to go alone? Do you need a hiking buddy or guide? What about going out at night? Remember, you can see and do all you want without risky behavior. Staying safe allows you to enjoy the trip!

- Use your common sense! Be safe, be smart, and trust your instincts. If you do not feel safe, grab a taxi or rickshaw to get to a safer place.

-Don't walk alone on a dark street at night - man or woman! Use your common sense.

-Trust your intuition - if something doesn't feel right, bail! Don't worry about what anyone else thinks - your safety is the most important thing!

-If you feel endangered, wave at someone nearby, shout greetings as if you know them, and run over to them.

-Cause a commotion! The person harassing you will likely leave you alone.

-The inhabitants of most countries treat tourists like gold, as tourism is a large part of their income.

-Be sure your hotel room door and windows are locked every time you leave the room, no matter how secure you feel. It doesn't take but a minute for someone (or maybe a monkey) to come in and rob you.

-Be sure when you use the ATM that no one is standing close. Use common sense always.

-Use taxis at night in areas you are not sure about. If you have to walk a short distance to get a taxi and the street looks deserted, walk in the middle of the street. It is harder for anyone to grab you from an alley, etc. Better safe than sorry!

-Give a copy of your itinerary to someone at home...just in case.

-When making friends with locals and other travelers, don't tell them the name of your hotel until you know them better. Remember, you just met. I have had men knock on my door late at night wanting in! Lesson learned!

-Limit alcohol intake and keep your wits about you!

-In today's world, one might want to take a face mask, anti-bacterial gel and hand wipes. Some restaurants have a wash basin in the dining room to wash your hands before dining.

Bangkok, Thailand

I share the following story as it is part of the adventure and a memorable event within my travels. I look back on it with some humor (a sense of humor must always be packed up and taken with you wherever you go). Happily, the outcome was good but the potential for what could have been a disaster remains clear in my memory.

It was my last night in Bangkok and my last minute shopping was complete. I headed back across the street to Khao San Road and my hotel. I had to be at the airport by 11 p.m., and it was now 8 p.m., so I needed to finish packing. As I crossed the first lane of traffic, there was a bus that was stopped for a light about 1/4 block to my left. I caught the bus driver's eye, then crossed in front of him and stopped on the center stripe. To my left, the light had changed and the traffic was slowly making its way toward me. Keeping my eye on the first car, I started across the street. What I didn't see was the motorcycle until it hit me. The driver was obviously tired of waiting behind the bus and decided to zip around it in the wrong lane.

Luckily, I was wearing a leather handbag which hung on my right shoulder. The fender of the bike put a 2" tear in the leather where it struck. If not for the bag, that would have been my hip! When the driver of the bike saw he was about to hit me, he laid the bike down sideways. It was like slow motion; I pushed myself across the side of the bike, trying to avoid the hot pipes, and rolled on the pavement. Frightening memories of an old bike accident when I had gotten severely burned on the exhaust pipes, flashed through my mind.

Much like a scene in an old movie, both the driver and I were angry, scared and hollering at each other, me in English, he in Thai. I had no idea what he said, nor did he understand me! My next realization was that his wife and little child were riding with him. I got up, quickly checked myself for any obvious signs of injuries, and hobbled over to the sidewalk to see if they were okay. Thankfully, and luckily for them, they were fine.

A crowd gathered, chattering. "We should call the Police!" "You should go to the hospital!" I asked another traveler to walk around me to double check if everything looked okay. "I'm not bleeding anywhere, am I?" I asked. "No, just a little road dirt", she assured me. I was quite shaken up but relieved that other than my dignity being bruised, and my leather bag torn, I was okay. I told them not to call the police; it would just make trouble for the driver of the motorcycle. And no, I didn't want to go to the hospital as I didn't really have time and I felt okay. Someone helped me to the sidewalk and gave me a juice to drink. I knew this whole episode would make for a good story, though at the time, I clearly was not amused! What could have been an awful disaster, turned out fine and hopefully the lesson learned for that motorcycle driver is that he needs to be more patient with buses and a lot more careful. As a pedestrian, extra caution should be exercised when crossing streets because some drivers are just plain unpredictable!

Chapter 8

Money Matters

"We have to continually be jumping off cliffs and developing our wings on the way down."
Kurt Vonnegut

You always hear the term "travel on a shoestring," but what does that mean? It means pinching pennies, foregoing expensive tours, using local transportation, and eating some meals in your room or on the street. Have a budget for each day.

-Do free things! Why pack your itinerary with expensive pursuits? Stroll bazaars, visit churches, gaze at the birds on the lake, hike the woods, free day at the museum, etc.

-ATMs are now available in most places and the exchange rate is better. Be sure to check your guidebook. Save your cash for towns where there are no ATMs.

-Take $30-$50 in $1 bills, U.S. currency, for those times when they cannot change large bills.

U.S. bills are accepted for exchange almost everywhere now.

-Make sure you get new bills from the bank - no tears or severe wear, as some foreign banks won't take them. You can even iron them!

-Before you leave, set up Bill Pay on your bank's website, especially if you are taking a long trip.

-You can use money exchanges in most airports, so you will have local currency for the taxi, etc. until you get to the ATM. They don't always give a good exchange rate, so don't exchange a lot here.

-Travel with no more than 2 credit cards - one on you and one at the hotel. Keep in mind that carrying multiple credit cards could be an invitation to thieves, especially in countries where there is a great deal of poverty. Every time you open your wallet, they see all those cards. Personal space is not the same as we experience at home. People are curious about foreigners and they watch everything you do.

-Take money for the day out of your money belt before you leave the room. The belt cannot protect your money if you are going in and out of it in public. Wear it *under* your clothes!

-Need a cheat sheet for the foreign exchange rate? You can print one at onanda.com.

-Sometimes you are only able to cash travelers checks in a bank. This limits you as to when you can get cash, as the bank may not be open when you need it. Since most places have ATMs, I no longer recommend travelers checks.

-After reaching your destination, you can put your money in a snack-size Ziploc bag to keep it from getting sweaty and dirty. Although money belts are water (or perspiration) resistant, that does not mean waterproof. In a hot and humid climate, you will definitely perspire through the part next to your skin. Put your passport toward the outside.

-Ask the price of a taxi/rickshaw ride before getting in so you can bargain.

-Everything is negotiable including hotel rooms, taxis, and most purchases. Develop your haggling skills by practicing before leaving home. You can try garage sales or flea markets.

-Remember, before you leave, to change your money back to your home currency. Or, you can take it to customer service at your bank, and they will change it to local currency and deposit it for you. No one takes coins, only bills. Perhaps

someone in your family collects coins or you can start your own collection!

Jaipur, India

When it comes to "travel woes," don't think for a moment that I don't have a story or two to tell! I share these with you so you can avoid some of the mistakes I made along the way. Sometimes simple common sense is the best way to avoid most travel hurdles, but usually it takes some extra attention to details to avoid big inconveniences.

Since I had been on an overnight train from Udaipur, I was wearing my money belt on the back of my waist for comfort (a no-no for obvious reasons). As I stood at the front desk of the hotel in Jaipur, India, I reached behind me to get my passport. Inadvertently, I must have dropped my ATM card on the floor at the same time.

The next day, I decided to go shopping and made my way to the nearest bank, at which time I discovered my ATM card was no longer in my money belt. I felt a surge of panic as I knew it was the only way I had to get money in India. I realized I committed the cardinal sin of not having two cards with me. I immediately returned to the hotel and inquired at the desk if anyone had found my card. With no luck, I rushed to the computer to email for money from the States. The irony was that I was just reading about the email scams from supposed friends and/or family stranded overseas asking for emergency funds! Finally I had a reply from my nephew. I managed to convince him that the email was really from me, so he wired enough money to hold me over until I could get a new card. On top of all this, I was anxious to change hotels because adding insult to injury, a mouse had run across my pillow the night before! EEK!

After calling the bank and reporting the missing card, I found that getting a replacement card was not that quick or easy. The only way to get another card would be to have it sent to my address on file, which of course, was in the States. After it arrived at my home, my nephew would then send it DHL to me. The process would take at least two weeks.

A little distraught, a lot inconvenienced, but luckily unscathed, I took a deep breath and decided my best option would be to go back to Udaipur for the two weeks until my card arrived. It would be a less expensive stay than in the larger city and to my good fortune, I had made friends there who invited me to stay with them while I awaited my new card. With some patience, gratitude, and a little help from my friends, an unfortunate situation was resolved - plus, there were some big lessons learned that day!

-Use caution when getting into my money belt - never in public.

-Carry two cards when traveling at all times, one with me, one left safely at the hotel.

-And always have a backup plan. Lesson learned!

Chapter 9

Food & Drink

"I am not a great cook, I am not a great artist, but I love art, and I love food, so I am the perfect traveler." *Michael Palin*

Although I tend to eat at street stalls because it's less expensive, it's not normally recommended. If you are adventurous, check the vendors' hygiene. Is the cook area clean? Do they handle money and then put their hands back in the food? I ate from the same vendor in Bangkok every day as his hygiene was good, the food was tasty, and a stir-fried dish cost less than a dollar.

- Check your guidebook for recommended eating places, but get out and look for yourself as well. In Latin America, a lot of places have a set menu for lunch (almuerza) for the local crowd, and it is usually more than you can eat (can be 3 courses) and for a cheap price. In general, look for places where the locals crowd in to eat - the food is good and the price is right!

-Purchase and carry a good water bottle that does not leak so you can throw it in your day pack or handbag. Always carry water! In a hot and/or dry climate, you should be drinking water constantly. If not, you will dehydrate before you know it. I learned this when I was training in the Peace Corps. Try to find places to re-fill your bottle for a small fee or ask the hotel if they have filtered water that you can use for refills. You save money and the environment!

-Keep snacks in your room for those late night munchies - biscuits/cookies, nuts, fruit, etc.

-Always take a water bottle and a snack when you leave your room. Who knows, you may run into something or someone and want to stay out longer.

-Be flexible and enjoy the quirky little nuances you may encounter. Once I had a small parrot walk around my table and eat the seeds from my watermelon as I ate it from my plate.

-Be open to new food experiences. At New Year's in Nicaragua, they serve baby goat at midnight. They go to the farmer, purchase a small goat, take it to the lady on the edge of town, and she bakes it in a large clay oven in her back yard. The meat was falling off the bone - delicious!

A Taste of India

Banana, Pumpkin, or Mango Curry

This curry is delicious with either pumpkin, mango, or firm bananas. I obtained this recipe at the Moon Cafe in Udaipur, Rajasthan, in northern India. It is super delicious and can be served with rice and flat bread.

Ingredients:

2 tbs. Ghee

1/2 tsp. Mustard seeds

Pinch Chili powder

1 whole Anise, crushed or 1/2 tsp. powder

1/2 tsp. Sugar

1/2 tsp. Fennel seeds

1/2 tsp. Coriander powder

1 tsp. Turmeric

Salt to taste

2 cups Banana, mango, or pumpkin cut in 1/2"
cubes

1 med. Tomato, chopped

1 small Onion, chopped small

Water as needed

Melt ghee in large skillet or wok shaped pan. Add
all spices and onion. Saute until the onion is
tender. Add tomato, and either banana, mango,
or pumpkin. Add water as needed and stir well.
Cover and cook 10 min. or until done. Enjoy!

Chapter 10

Communications

"Certain travelers give the impression that they keep moving because only then do they feel fully alive." *Ella Maillart*

While it may sound silly, I miss the days when I could go to South America and get lost - no one could find me! Such freedom.... While today you may want to stay in touch with friends and family through email and social media, you miss something by not being able to fully immerse yourself in the local culture. You may want to try doing your email less often and gain a more authentic experience.

- If planning to carry a phone, will it work overseas? Do you need to get it unlocked so you can use a foreign SIM card? If you are not under contract, but are using a phone service provider, they will tell you how to unlock it. You can also buy unlocked phones on eBay.com or carry an old phone that is unlocked.

-Take a photo of your new friends with your phone and attach it to their contact info. It will make it easier to remember them.

-If you have a smart phone, or WiFi-enabled tablet, you can get an application that allows you to call anyone, anywhere in the world for free. Try Viber (a smart phone app) for calls & texts, WhatsApp (another app) for texts & voice messages, or with Skype, you can call at a greatly reduced price if not free. With all these, the person you are contacting needs to have the same app on their phone, tablet, or computer. If they don't, there will be a charge.

-Look for hotels that have WiFi, even if it is only in the restaurant or lobby. If not, eat out at a restaurant that has it. This will save paying for it at an internet cafe.

-Write addresses for postcards in the back of your journal rather than carry an address book. You can also print them on labels, then you will know when you have sent them all. In this age of technology it is still nice to receive a post card from another country!

-You need passport-size photos for a visa when crossing borders, buying a SIM card, and most official documents. In most countries, you can get photos done at a fraction of the price you would pay at home. For instance, in India I got eight photos for less than the price of one at home!

Chapter 11

Blogs & Journals

"It is better to travel well than to arrive." *Buddha*

What is a "blog"? "Blog" is an abbreviated version of "weblog," which is a term used to describe web sites that maintain an ongoing chronicle of information. The beauty of a blog is the documentation of all the exciting and fascinating experiences you have in your travels. Blogging is about impressions and feelings; it is not a guide. So, when writing yours, tell about the impression a place or person had on you. What made you smile? How did you feel looking at that pyramid, climbing those ruins, seeing the Taj Mahal, or having a monkey grab your leg?

Blog:

Don't feel like you have to have a blog. Many people are doing them, but it is not a pre-requisite to travel. Only do a blog if you enjoy it.

-Use photos to enhance your story. Place people in the photo to emphasize the size and/or grandeur of a place or building. Learn to take selfies!

-List the web address of your blog on your Facebook page for more readers. Send an email, with your blog address, to friends so they can keep up with your trip.

-Make it a pleasure, not a chore! Write when you can, not necessarily every day, so it remains an enjoyable activity. Sometimes I only write one post per town.

-There are several sites that allow you to make a free blog. I use blogger.com, a part of Google, but there are several others.

Journal:

Your personal journal is a place to put down those personal feelings and events, which may not be something you want to share. After all, this is your journal and it can hold your personal thoughts.

- Journal daily, even if it is only a few lines, so you

don't lose momentum. Try doing it at the same time daily, maybe during breakfast or before bed.

- Make lists in it - a proposed itinerary, what you brought with you (packing list), what you wish you had taken (refine your packing list when you return), record favorite recipes, names of people you met, a postage stamp from the country visited, saved ticket stubs, names of hotels including cost and room number so you can review them on tripadvisor.com.

Blog Entry

May 24, 2014 Kullu to Kasol

I took the local bus south to Bhuntar, where I made my connection for Kasol in the northern part of the Parvati Valley, in northern India. It is the next to last town on the road with only a few small villages to the northeast. The sign on the bus read:

33% seats for ledies (ladies)

10% seats for children under 14 yrs.

5% seats for senior citizens

NO OVERLOAD ALLOWED!

I was grateful for my window seat, as the school children and locals (from the country) piled onto the bus, filling all the seats and aisles. As we climbed in altitude, I viewed the snow-capped Himalayan Mountains and it reminded me of the fact that with each change of towns, I was going higher in altitude. Wild roses grow everywhere, mixing white with the many shades of green. I arrived in Kasol 3-1/2 hrs. later.

I checked into the Turquoise Cafe & Lodge, which offered a nice room with a private balcony, directly above the roaring rapids of a tributary to the Parvati River. I all but lived on this balcony for two weeks and watched the activities of the local people. The sound of the river was a constant presence and conducive to writing, relaxing, and sleeping. Many days I sat at the marble-top table on the balcony, listening to the river and typing. The owner of the hotel, Pratibha, and I became great friends and shared time and tea many days. We still keep in touch, but I will miss seeing her.

There was a small shanty town on the opposite bank of the river. I observed their lifestyle as they gathered all the plastic water bottles in huge bags, hauled them down to their "yard" where they crushed and re-bagged them for hauling to the recycling facility to sell. I find the Indian people to be very resourceful in finding ways to live when they have no resources. I often thought that a trash system would be great for the environment. As it is, they sweep it up in the street and burn it, or dump it down the banks of the river.

Kasol is known as the well-established hippie hangout of this valley. Both the Kullu and Parvati Valleys are known for their quality marijuana, which is not the same as the wild hemp that grows along the roads and rivers. The tourists consist mainly of Israeli youth who were recently released from the army and are ready to party. The rest are a mixture of Indian and western tourists, and other travelers.

The birds soared high overhead, over the tall pines in this high mountain valley. Ravens...lots of them! They kept the town picked clean of edible waste, both on land and water. Every creature has its purpose in nature.

The hiking trails were well maintained as the locals made use of them in their daily lives. As I hiked, I observed a man with a small herd of pack animals, both horses and donkeys, taking a nap under an overhanging rock; animals were tethered and pack saddles thrown aside. This was more proof of the laid back lifestyle of this forested haven.

Chapter 12

Off the Beaten Path - Adventurers Only!

"Certainly, travel is more than the seeing of sights; it is a change that goes on, deep and permanent, in the ideas of living." *Mary Ritter Beard*

Off the beaten path is exactly what it sounds like - maybe a bit quirky, a lot interesting, and definitely not mainstream touristy. This is for the hardcore adventurer - travelers, not tourists! Here are a few reasons why and tips to try:

-It is less expensive. Out of the way places don't attract as many westerners and the prices have not gone up. Once the infrastructure is well in place, so are the prices.

-Adventure is usually not comfortable and convenient. Sanitation is different, and you may have to take cold baths. Try bathing mid-afternoon when the room has warmed a bit.

-You will meet fewer tourists because some places are not really equipped for tourism as in hotels, language, etc., and it can be a challenge to find people who speak English, or to find a place to stay. For instance, I saw no tourists at the Suez Canal and I only met one person who spoke English. It made it difficult so I only stayed two days, explored the area, then left.

-There are opportunities for more adventure because everything is a challenge, inspiring you to be creative and resourceful in solving the challenges as they appear.

- Seek off-beat accommodations -

Convents and monasteries are usually found on the internet, and some in guidebooks. They can be free at times, but expect basic accommodations and to go by their rules; it is a holy place. You will need to contact them to arrange this type of stay.

Home-stays are in guidebooks and are also found through the tourist bureau. This is not the same as home exchange. A home-stay is a room in a local family's home.

Couchsurfing.org is a service that connects members to a global community of travelers. Use Couchsurfing to find a place to stay, or share your "couch" and hometown with travelers. Their motto: "We envision a world made better by travel and travel made richer by connection. Couchsurfers share their lives with the people they encounter, fostering cultural exchange and mutual respect."

-Take a walking, bicycle, or camel tour. One lady bought a horse and traveled horseback in the country she was in for several months, then sold the horse when she was ready to leave! Don't ask me how she managed to feed it, etc.

-Take a freighter! While cruise ships are organized for tourists, freighters are made to haul freight. However, they do have rooms available for people who can entertain themselves and are not expecting haute cuisine.

-While I don't recommend it, you can also hitchhike. This can be dangerous and I really do not encourage women to try this. Taking a ride from someone you know is different.

-Volunteer! Sometimes they have a room for you, and you may only have to pay for food. Sometimes they charge you an exorbitant amount plus you have to pay your own airfare. These are called "volunteer vacations". With a little research, you can find places that really need the help and do not charge at all. Normally these are discovered after arrival in the country although I have found some online.

I was on my way to Nepal and found a website that offers volunteer opportunities in orphanages worldwide (see Resources for link). This could be ideal for a long-term visit.

Chapter 13

Women's Travel Tips

"One travels more usefully when alone, because he reflects more." *Thomas Jefferson*

If you have been waiting to find the right person to go along on your trip, look in the mirror, then get out your passport! Women who hesitated for years before traveling solo have an almost universal response during their first solo trip - "Why did I wait so long to do this?" By forfeiting the support of a companion, you open yourself up to the support of the whole world. And you don't want to be one of the herd that gets on the bus at 4 a.m. to arrive at the next place, get off to take a photo, then back on the bus for the next stop and repeat. When I was in Luxor, Egypt, I watched about 35 people get off a tour bus and be literally herded down the street to their hotel. I was glad I was not one of them.

- A cruise may be a more comfortable way to begin solo travel. It is relatively safe, with meals, entertainment, and accommodations provided.

This is tourist travel, but a good way to get acquainted with foreign or solo travel. If you are a true traveler at heart, your interest in other cultures will not be satisfied by short land excursions from cruise ships. It will leave you wanting more.

-If you feel self-conscious dining alone, sit at the bar. Some places have long communal tables that can be fun and a good way to meet others. Or take a book to read or journal at that time.

-Wearing a wedding ring will help fend off the Romeos, whether you are married or not.

-If you use tampons, bring a supply as they may only sell sanitary napkins.

-Keep your bag in sight at all times! When dining, do not put it on the floor or the back of your chair. Anyone can lift it without you knowing. I hang it on my knee, put it in my lap, or next to me in my chair. At train or bus stations, stand or sit with your large pack between your knees and the smaller one on your lap. My friend, while waiting on a train, was asked by a young man for the time. While she was distracted to her left, another one came from her right side and got her entire large backpack!

- When sight-seeing, walk with purpose, head up,

not looking at a map. Check your map before leaving the hotel, or pop into a store or cafe to check it again.

- Worried about getting sick and being alone? You can get a doctor to your room, or if you do not need a doctor, ask the front desk or restaurant to send you water and/or meals while you recuperate in your room. People are generally very helpful when you are sick, especially if you are a woman traveling alone.

Goa, India

Traveling solo has some heartwarming surprises. I discovered that people, no matter what culture, can be incredibly kind and caring.

It was winter in the north of India where I had been traveling and I had contracted a lung infection. I decided to go south to the beach where it was warm. After a long and arduous overnight bus trip from Udaipur to Ahmedabad, four hours in the airport, a short flight to Goa, and finally a bus trip of seven hours to Palolem Beach, I arrived and settled into my hotel room.

Morning came and I could barely get out of bed. I made my way downstairs to the front desk. The owner of the hotel saw that I was obviously quite sick and offered to get a rickshaw to take me to the doctor. However I was feeling way too weak and ill to go anywhere. Without hesitation, he got on his motorcycle and went to get the medical help I needed. Within 15 minutes, an English-speaking doctor arrived at my room. After an exam, the doctor reported that I had a high fever and was on the verge of pneumonia. He wrote two prescriptions, and advised me to stay in bed for the next 2-3 days. The manager of the hotel promptly got back on his bike and drove to the next town, where they had a pharmacy, for my medication.

For the next few days, this kind hotel manager sent his daughter to get meals for me three times a day. I remain deeply grateful, for I don't know what I would have done without the kindness and consideration of this dear man and his daughter. While I didn't get to the beach until the last day, thanks to this man, I fully recovered, I avoided a severe illness, and I was once again well enough to travel. People are so helpful when, as a woman, you travel alone!

Chapter 14

Personal Maintenance

"To awaken quite alone in a strange town is one
of the pleasantest sensations in the world."
Freya Stark

It can be challenging to stay groomed on the road,
especially for women. Here are some tips:

-You can try local places to get a haircut, or cut it
in a style that can grow out gracefully while you
are away from home.

-Take a small manicure kit, or clippers and a file.
If you only have a carry-on and were unable to
bring your own due to regulations on metal items,
you can probably get these at a pharmacy or a
salon after arriving.

-A blow dryer is very helpful for not only looking
your best, but to keep you from having to go out
in the cold with a wet head. Remember,
electricity voltage can be different in other
countries. While the U.S. is 110, South America
and many others are 210-240. You can get a

small, folding, travel dryer with a button to switch between the two. Another option is to buy a dryer online with a plug that fits the sockets in the country you are visiting. See the Resources page for a website.

-Wearing socks with sandals may look nerdy, but you need to protect your feet. Serious travel is not about fashion! Your sandals may also be a welcome change to hiking boots after a long day hiking or sightseeing, or shopping all day in enclosed shoes.

-Stay in shape by doing yoga and/or crunches for your abs. While you may be walking a lot, don't forget about keeping your core strong. You can also go to a gym or take yoga classes in the town you are visiting. It can be a fun way to interact with the locals and meet other travelers.

-Carry your own toilet paper. Most third world establishments do not supply paper; in some countries they do not use it at all. The more remote the area, the less likely it is that you will even be able to buy any - always carry your own. If you put a roll without the core in a Ziploc bag, you can pull it from the middle without having to remove it from the bag. This really comes in handy in some of the more primitive toilets.

Chapter 15

Books & Films

"The world is a book, and those who do not travel read only a page." *Saint Augustine*

Learn a bit about the country you are to visit through films and books. I have read a lot of these books, both on the road and before I left for my trip, and found them very inspiring. You can also get wonderful documentaries and travel films at the public library.

Books:

Dreams of the Heart: *President Violeta Barrios de Chamorro* of Nicaragua

Passionate Nomad - *Jane Fletcher*

A Journey of One's Own - *Thalia Zepatos*

The Alchemist - *Paul Cohelo*

Shantaram - *Gregory David Roberts*

94

White Tiger - *Aravind Adiga*

The Space Between Us - *Thrity Umrigar*

Amazing Traveler: *Isabelle Bird*

Blood River: The Terrifying Journey Through the World's Most Dangerous Country - *Tim Butcher*

Tales of a Female Nomad: Living at Large in the World - *Rita Golden Gelman*

One Hundred Years of Solitude - *Gabriel Garcia Marquez*

Tracks - *Robyn Davidson*

Travels in West Africa - *Mary Kingsley*

My Journey in Lhasa - *Alexandra David-Neel*

Midnight's Children - *Salman Rushdie*

Films:

Asia/India:

Monsoon Wedding - *India*

Earth - *India*

Water - India

Fire - *India*

Gandhi - *India*

The Best Exotic Marigold Hotel - *India*

The Scent of Green Papaya - *Vietnam*

The Killing Fields - *Cambodia*

The Last Emperor - *China*

Raise the Red Lantern - *China*

North Africa/Middle East:

Under the Sheltering Sky - *North Africa*

Hideous Kinky - *Morocco*

Death on the Nile - *Egypt*

Children of Heaven - *Iran*

The Kite Runner - *Iran*

Africa:

Blood Diamond - *Africa*

Out of Africa - *Africa*

The English Patient - *Africa*

Lawrence of Arabia - *Africa*

Hideous Kinky - *Morocco*

Central & South America:

The Motorcycle Diaries - *South America*

The Art of Travel - *Nicaragua*

Love in the Time of Cholera - *Columbia*

La Menacing - *Argentina*

Australia:

Muriel's Wedding - *Australia*

The Rabbit Fence - *Australia*

Walkabout - *Australia*

Eastern Europe/Russia:

The Unbearable Lightness of Being - *Czech Republic*

Everything is Illuminated - *Russia*

Anna Karenina - *Russia*

Chapter 16

Resources

Here are a few websites I use regularly to save as much money as possible:

tripadvisor.com - Great for reviews of places to stay and restaurants. You will want to give them your own reviews upon return home.

world-import.com/plugs.htm - plug adapters and converters

onanda.com - Money exchange rates and charts you can print

indiamike.com - All you need to know about India including the train system. If you join (free) you can ask questions on their extensive forums.

amazon.com - Discounted guidebooks, and all sorts of travel stuff. Note: Lonely Planet has changed their format and you may want to check out the new one before purchasing.

eBay.com - I went to the shoe store before I left home, tried on the sandals I wanted, and got them for much less on eBay by knowing the size, model number, and name. You can do this with all type of travel items as well.

kayak.com - Flights, hotels, etc. If you click the box for "Flexible Dates", it will show you a monthly calendar with the price for each day's flights.

priceline.com - You can bid on flights, hotels, and cars, but you trade your choice of airlines, times, layovers, etc. for more savings.

couchsurfing.org - Stay in a local's home for 1-3 days! It is a great way to learn the culture, and some of them can show you around. Read the profiles carefully before you choose. Women may want to stay with other women or families. Don't expect a lot of privacy.

bookingbuddy.com - Easy to use to book hostels, hotels, & guesthouses

hostelbookers.com - Good for hostel booking and other hotels

skyscanner.com - Also searches smaller airlines for lower prices on flights

indianeagle.com - An airline for good domestic fares in India *cleartrip.com* - Planes, trains (limited to India), hotels

cellphoneshop.com - This is in China, so whatever you order you will need to give it plenty of time to arrive. They have inexpensive unlocked phones, including smart phones, cases for all electronics, cords, etc.

twitter.com - Travel bargains at #traveldeals and follow @thepointsguy - he finds amazing deals!

freevolunteering.co.uk/index - Volunteer for free in countries around the world

City Passes - Some larger cities have these and they are a real money saver. For example, for Paris go to parispass.com

Blogs:

There are so many! If you do not find what you want here, you can do a search for "solo women travel blog".

gainesbishop.com - Bras in the Backpack: Solo Travel Tips - learn more travel tips, read and submit travel tales. Read my blog about India!

thevagabond.com - Solo female travel blog

journeywoman.com - Travel resources for women

wanderlustandlipstick.com - Tips and tales of solo women travelers

solotravelerblog.com - For solo women travelers

thatbackpacker.com - From a girl who travels full-time

Travelettes.net - Has good information on a variety of destinations

Currency Around the World

U.S.A.	dollar
Mexico	peso
Guatemala	quetzal
Honduras	lempira
Nicaragua	cordoba
Costa Rica	colón
Panama	US Dollar, balboa
Columbia	Columbian peso
Ecuador	U.S. dollar
Peru	nuevo sol
Bolivia	boliviano
India	rupee
Thailand	baht
Cambodia	riel
Vietnam	dong
Nepal	Nepalese Rupee
Egypt	Egyptian pound
Jordan	Jordanian dinar
Czech Repub.	koruna

Centigrade or Fahrenheit?

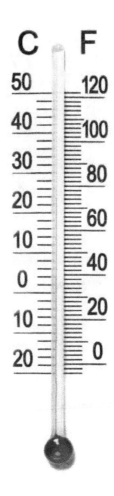

Author: *Gaines Bishop*

Profile on Smashwords:
smashwords.com/profile/view/gabish45

Smashwords Interview:
smashwords.com/interview/gabish45

India Blog:
gaines-indianepal.blogspot.com